EUROPEAN COUNTRIES TODAY
GERMANY

EUROPEAN COUNTRIES TODAY

TITLES IN THE SERIES

Austria	Italy
Belgium	Netherlands
Czech Republic	Poland
Denmark	Portugal
France	Spain
Germany	Sweden
Greece	United Kingdom
Ireland	European Union Facts & Figures

EUROPEAN COUNTRIES TODAY
GERMANY

Dominic J. Ainsley

MASON CREST

Mason Crest
450 Parkway Drive, Suite D
Broomall, Pennsylvania PA 19008
(866) MCP-BOOK (toll free)

Copyright © 2019 by Mason Crest, an imprint of National Highlights, Inc. All rights reserved. No part of this publication may be reproduced or transmitted in any form or by any means, electronic or mechanical, including photocopying, recording, taping, or any information storage and retrieval system, without permission in writing from the publisher.

First printing
9 8 7 6 5 4 3 2 1

ISBN: 978-1-4222-3984-1
Series ISBN: 978-1-4222-3977-3
ebook ISBN: 978-1-4222-7799-7

Cataloging-in-Publication Data on file with the Library of Congress.

Printed in the United States of America

Cover images
Main: *The town of Cochem on the river Rhine.*
Left: *Pretzels and beer.*
Center: *Frankfurt am Main.*
Right: *The Oktoberfest in Munich.*

QR CODES AND LINKS TO THIRD-PARTY CONTENT

You may gain access to certain third-party content ("Third-Party Sites") by scanning and using the QR Codes that appear in this publication (the "QR Codes"). We do not operate or control in any respect any information, products, or services on such Third-Party Sites linked to by us via the QR Codes included in this publication, and we assume no responsibility for any materials you may access using the QR Codes. Your use of the QR Codes may be subject to terms, limitations, or restrictions set forth in the applicable terms of use or otherwise established by the owners of the Third-Party Sites. Our linking to such Third-Party Sites via the QR Codes does not imply an endorsement or sponsorship of such Third-Party Sites or the information, products, or services offered on or through the Third-Party Sites, nor does it imply an endorsement or sponsorship of this publication by the owners of such Third-Party Sites.

CONTENTS

	Germany at a Glance	6
Chapter 1	Germany's Geography & Landscape	11
Chapter 2:	The Government & History of Germany	23
Chapter 3:	The German Economy	43
Chapter 4:	Citizens of Germany: People, Customs & Culture	53
Chapter 5:	The Famous Cities of Germany	65
Chapter 6:	A Bright Future for Germany	83
	Chronology	90
	Further Reading & Internet Resources	91
	Index	92
	Picture Credits & Author	96

KEY ICONS TO LOOK FOR:

Words to Understand: These words with their easy-to-understand definitions will increase the reader's understanding of the text while building vocabulary skills.

Sidebars: This boxed material within the main text allows readers to build knowledge, gain insights, explore possibilities, and broaden their perspectives by weaving together additional information to provide realistic and holistic perspectives.

Educational Videos: Readers can view videos by scanning our QR codes, providing them with additional content to supplement the text. Examples include news coverage, moments in history, speeches, iconic sports moments, and much more!

Text-Dependent Questions: These questions send the reader back to the text for more careful attention to the evidence presented there.

Research Projects: Readers are pointed toward areas of further inquiry connected to each chapter. Suggestions are provided for projects that encourage deeper research and analysis.

GERMANY AT A GLANCE

MAP OF EUROPE

The Geography of Germany

Location: Central Europe, bordering the North and Baltic Seas, between the Netherlands and Poland, south of Denmark

Area: slightly smaller than Montana
total: 137,846 square miles (357,022 sq. km)
land: 134,623 square miles (348,672 sq. km)
water: 3,223 square miles (8,350 sq. km)

Borders: Austria 497 miles (801 km), Belgium 82 miles (133 km), Czech Republic 437 miles (704 km), Denmark 42 miles (86 km), France 259 miles (418 km), Luxembourg 79 miles (128 km), Netherlands 357 miles (575 km), Poland 290 miles (467 km), Switzerland 216 miles (348 km)

Climate: temperate; cool, cloudy, wet winters and summers; more extreme temperatures inland; south, a colder region

Terrain: lowlands in north, uplands in center, mountains in south

Elevation Extremes:
Lowest point: Neuendorf bei Wilster -11.6 feet (-3.54 meters)
Highest point: Zugspitze 9,719 feet (2,963 meters)

Natural Hazards: flooding

Source: www.cia.gov 2017

GERMANY AT A GLANCE

Flag of Germany

Germany stretches from the North and Baltic Seas in the north to the Alps in the south. The reunification of East and West Germany in 1990 caused many problems, not least the huge cost of reconstruction. Since those challenging times, however, Germany has risen to be a financially strong country and the most successful exporting nation in the European Union. The new Germany not only retained the name, the Federal Republic of Germany, but also kept the original West German flag, the red, black, and gold colors dating from the days of the Holy Roman Empire.

ABOVE: *People enjoying lunch in Heidelberg, Baden-Württemberg. The city is a popular tourist destination due to its picturesque cityscape and castle.*

EUROPEAN COUNTRIES TODAY: GERMANY

The People of Germany

Population: 80,594,017
Ethnic Groups: German 91.5%, Turkish 2.4%, other 6.1%
Age Structure:
    0–14 years: 12.82%
    15–64 years: 65.12%
    65 years and over: 22.06%
Population Growth Rate: 0.02 %
Birth Rate: 8.6 births/1,000 population
Death Rate: 11.7 deaths/1,000 population
Migration Rate: 1.5 migrant(s)/1,000 population
Infant Mortality Rate: 4.2 deaths/1,000 live births
Life Expectancy at Birth:
    Total Population: 80.7 years
    Male: 78.4 years
    Female: 83.1 years
Total Fertility Rate: 1.45 children born/woman
Religions: Protestant 27%, Roman Catholic 29%,
    Muslim 4.4%, unaffiliated or other 39.6%
Languages: German
Literacy Rate: 99%

Source: www.cia gov 2017

Words to Understand

cultivation: The planting, tending, or harvesting of crops.

gorges: Narrow clefts or canyons with steep sides, especially those through which a stream runs.

temperate: Moderate in respect to temperature; not subject to prolonged extremes of hot or cold weather.

ABOVE: St. Trudpert's Abbey in Münstertal in the southern Black Forest, Baden-Württemberg. Although it used to be a Benedictine monastery, today it is home to the Sisters of St. Joseph of St. Trudpert.

Chapter One
GERMANY'S GEOGRAPHY & LANDSCAPE

Guten Tag! Welcome to Germany, the "Pivot of Europe." Situated right in the heart of Europe, Germany has historically functioned as a crossroads for many peoples, ideas, and even armies. Now it provides a natural gateway connecting its traditional Western European trading partners to the fast-growing Central and East European economies.

Germany is the seventh-largest country in Europe. About the size of the state of Montana, it covers an area of 137,846 square miles (357,022 sq. kilometers). Nine nations and two seas make up Germany's borders. The North Sea, Denmark, and the Baltic Sea lie to the north. Poland and the Czech Republic border Germany to the east. The countries of Austria and Switzerland form the southern border, while France, Belgium, the Netherlands, and Luxembourg line Germany's western border. Several islands in the North and Baltic Seas are also included in Germany's territory.

The Landscape: Plains, Mountains, Valleys, and Forests

Germany is a relatively large country. It boasts a landscape of remarkable diversity. Stretching from coastal plains to mountain ranges, Germany can be divided into three major natural land regions: lowlands in the north, uplands in the center, and mountains in the south.

The North German Plain is a low, flatland mass that lies along and between the North and Baltic Seas, extending southward into eastern Germany. Marshlands, dunes, fjords, and tidal flats—which are nearly flat coastal areas, alternately covered and exposed by the tides—mark the German coast.

Wide river valleys cut through the North German Plain, providing soft, fertile land for **cultivation**. The farmland of the plain's eastern end is so fertile it has

GERMANY'S GEOGRAPHY & LANDSCAPE

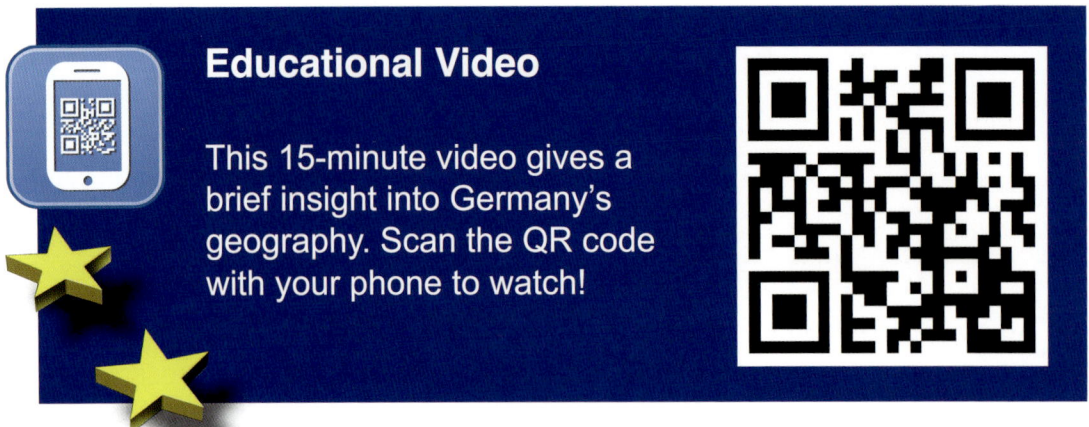

Educational Video

This 15-minute video gives a brief insight into Germany's geography. Scan the QR code with your phone to watch!

been dubbed Germany's breadbasket. Large ports and industrial centers have also developed along the riverbanks. Between the river valleys lie the heathlands—large areas covered with sand and gravel deposited by ancient glaciers. Heather, a low-growing shrub, flourishes in the heathlands' thin soil.

South of the North German Plain are the highlands of central Germany. These uplands are a striking terrain of low mountains, narrow valleys, and small basins. The highest points in central Germany are the Harz Mountains and the Thuringian Forest. Many rivers flow through the region, cutting rugged **gorges** through its hills. Grapes grow along the rivers' hillsides. In some places, the narrow river valleys widen into small basins that provide excellent farmland. The rivers are navigable, which has led to intensive industrial development in the region.

Germany's southern region includes the South German Hills, the Black Forest, and the Bavarian Alps. The region's earlier settlers were engaged primarily in agriculture and tourism. However, since the 1970s, industry has also developed here.

Long parallel ridges called escarpments cross the landscape of the South German Hills. Sheep are raised on these rocky ridges. The lowlands between the ridges contain some of Germany's best farmland.

In the southwest corner of Germany is the well-known Black Forest. This mountainous region, the scene of many old German legends and fairy tales,

EUROPEAN COUNTRIES TODAY: GERMANY

ABOVE: *Westerheversand Lighthouse on the North Sea coast is situated in the Schleswig-Holstein Wadden Sea National Park.*

13

GERMANY'S GEOGRAPHY & LANDSCAPE

The Black Forest

The Black Forest, (*Schwarzwald*), is an ancient mountain range in the state of Baden-Württemberg in southwestern Germany. It is the source of the Danube and Neckar rivers. Its highest peak is the Feldberg with an elevation of 4,898 feet (1,493 meters).

The vast area of hills, valleys, rivers, and forests stretch from the exclusive spa town of Baden-Baden to the Swiss border, and from the Rhine almost to Lake Constance.

derives its name from the dark fir and spruce trees found there. Small villages nestle in the forest. The region is famous for its delicious foods, especially its ham and chocolate-cherry cake.

In Germany's southeast corner, on its border with Austria, is Bavaria. This is where the Alpine mountains begin. The highest point in Germany, the 9,719-foot (2,963-meter) peak Zugspitze, is located here. The Bavarian Alps offer fantastic skiing, snowboarding, and sledding.

Rivers and Lakes

Germany claims more than 4,316 miles (6,950 kilometers) of interconnected rivers, canals, and lakes. Over the centuries, great cities have developed along these water routes.

The most important river is the Rhine. Both a tourist river and a busy transport waterway, it forms part of the borders with Switzerland and France

EUROPEAN COUNTRIES TODAY: GERMANY

ABOVE: *The town of Bingen on the river Rhine, Rhineland-Palatinate.*

GERMANY'S GEOGRAPHY & LANDSCAPE

before flowing into the Netherlands. The Elbe is another river crucial to German industry and agriculture. The Danube, Main, Neckar, Ems, Oder, and Weser are other important rivers.

Germany is dotted with picturesque lakes. The largest is Bodensee (Lake Constance), which lies partly in Austria and Switzerland. The glaciers that shaped the land in the last ice age have left behind many small lakes as well.

ABOVE: *View of Bodensee (Lake Constance) with the Alps in the background.*

EUROPEAN COUNTRIES TODAY: GERMANY

ABOVE: *Kaub in Rhineland-Palatinate. The temperate climate of the Rhine Valley provides the perfect climate for vineyards.*

A Temperate Climate

Germany has a cool, **temperate** climate with abundant rainfall and a long, overcast season. Because of their proximity to the sea, the northern lowlands enjoy an especially mild climate. The temperature in the north rarely dips below 30°F (-1°C) in the winter and averages about 64°F (18°C) during the summer.

Temperature ranges increase somewhat in the uplands of central and southern Germany. The warmest summer temperatures are in the Rhine valley and the coldest winter temperatures are in the Alps of the far south. The south also receives the heaviest precipitation, about 78 inches (198 centimeters) per year, much of it in the form of snow. The central uplands get about 20 inches (51 centimeters) of precipitation per year, and the lowlands in the north receive about 28 inches (71 centimeters) per year.

GERMANY'S GEOGRAPHY & LANDSCAPE

ABOVE: Once extinct in Germany, the Eurasian wolf has repopulated the countryside. It has spread from eastern Europe and the country now has approximately 400 wolves in residence. This photograph was taken in the Bavarian National Park.

EUROPEAN COUNTRIES TODAY: GERMANY

European Badger

The badger is a striking animal. Most apparent are the two black stripes that run the length of its white face. This marking acts as a signal to warn off predators. This short-legged omnivore has powerful legs and strong claws, making it an exceptional digger. It excavates an extensive system of burrows called a sett. The sett is made up of tunnels and chambers, sometimes occupying several levels.

Badgers are active during dawn and dusk and also at night, emerging to forage, groom themselves, and play with other members of the group. The badger has a keen sense of smell and uses this sense to identify other individuals and their territories. In winter, they are much less active and their body temperature may fall slightly, but they do not properly hibernate and emerge to forage in mild weather. They feed on a wide variety of plants and animals. These include invertebrates such as earthworms, insects, snails, and slugs.

Trees, Plants, and Wildlife

About one-fourth of Germany is covered with woodlands. Most of the forests are in the south. While nearly a third of the forest cover is mixed, deciduous woodland, over two-thirds is composed of pine, fir, larch, and other conifers growing at higher altitudes. Beech, oak, and walnut trees are the main types of trees found in the lower woodlands. The Alpine region bursts with wildflowers. Berries and mushrooms also grow in abundance.

GERMANY'S GEOGRAPHY & LANDSCAPE

ABOVE: *The Eurasian lynx was extinct in Germany by 1850. However, it was reintroduced to the Bavarian Forest and the Harz in the 1990s. Other areas were populated by lynx moving in from neighboring countries. In 2002, the first birth of a wild lynx in Germany was announced. A litter was produced from a pair in the Harz National Park.*

EUROPEAN COUNTRIES TODAY: GERMANY

Germany's wildlife includes deer, wild boars, hares, weasels, badgers, wolves, and foxes. The adder is a poisonous snake found here. Finches, geese, and other migratory birds cross the country. Herring, cod, flounder, and ocean perch inhabit the coastal waters. The Alps are home to the snow hare, the alpine marmot, and the golden eagle.

The country is also home to endangered species such as the Eurasian otter and lynx. Germany maintains ninety nature parks, thirteen biosphere reserves, and thirteen national parks.

Text-Dependent Questions

1. Which two seas lie to the north of Germany?

2. Where is Bavaria?

3. Name one of Germany's endangered species.

Research Project

Write an essay on the regions of Germany and how they differ from each other from a geographical perspective.

Words to Understand

artifact: An object showing human workmanship from a particular period.

cultural: Relating to a particular group of people and their habits and traditions.

dictator: One ruling in an absolute or oppressive way.

BELOW: Neuschwanstein Castle near the village of Hohenschwangau in southwestern Bavaria. It was built in the nineteenth century in the Romanesque Revival architectural style.

Chapter Two
THE GOVERNMENT & HISTORY OF GERMANY

The country of Germany has not always existed in the form we see today. For centuries, the area was more of a **cultural** region than a nation. It was comprised of many territories, each fairly independent and ruled by its own leader. The people of these territories were culturally similar, but they were not united under one government. In 1871, these territories came together under a single government, and Germany the nation-state was born. However, the borders of this first nation-state, are not Germany's borders today. Within a century, the infant nation acquired a dark history: two world wars, a famous **dictator** and his terrible crimes, several rebellions, and the division of the country. Today, the Federal Republic of Germany stands as a united, democratic country, a leading member of the United Nations, and a central member of in the European Union (EU). As a nation, Germany is committed to peace and shares good relations with other countries. However, it has traveled a long road to reach its current state.

Ancient Germany

Ancient **artifacts** discovered on German lands indicate the area was home to early human beings 400,000 years ago. The Celts, however, were the first recorded people of the territory. Around 1000 BCE, north European tribes began migrating to the area. By 100 BCE, they had conquered the Celts and taken over the land completely.

The Romans dubbed these tribes *Germani*, and the land became known as Germania. The Germanic tribes were mostly farmers and hunters. The Romans called them barbarians and tried to push the Germani back, but after losing a major battle in 9 CE, the Romans instead started building barriers to keep them out. Slowly, the Roman Empire collapsed, and then it was the tribes' turn to plunder Rome. The western portion of the Roman Empire came under

THE GOVERNMENT & HISTORY OF GERMANY

Educational Video

An informative video about the Holy Roman Empire.

Germanic control in the 400s and was carved into tribal kingdoms.

The Franks emerged as the most powerful tribe in the region. Charlemagne, a Frank and the greatest ruler of the era, built an empire that extended over Germany, France, and much of central Italy. Civil wars followed Charlemagne's death, and his sons divided their father's empire into three kingdoms.

The Holy Roman Empire

Eventually, the Frankish dynasty died out in Germany and gave way to the Saxons. Otto I, a strong Saxon king, was crowned Holy Roman Emperor in 962 CE. The Holy Roman Empire, (not to be confused with the Roman Empire, BCE 31–476 CE), is often called the First German Reich; that is, the first German Empire. However, it was neither fully German nor a proper empire.

ABOVE: *Charlemagne by Albrecht Dürer.*

EUROPEAN COUNTRIES TODAY: GERMANY

ABOVE: *A replica of the Magdeburger Reiter, which depicts King Otto I. The original dates from the thirteenth century.*

THE GOVERNMENT & HISTORY OF GERMANY

The Holy Roman Empire was a group of western and central European territories that stood united in their Christianity. While there was one supreme emperor, each territory had its own individual ruler. Constant struggles between these rulers and the empire marked the period. The crown and the Roman Catholic Church were also locked in a power struggle.

In the early stages of the empire, the emperors were very powerful. But as time passed, they were forced to grant more and more power to territorial rulers. The feudal system became stronger. The nobility, a new class that challenged the emperor, emerged.

At its peak, the empire contained most of the territory that makes up today's Germany, Austria, Slovenia, Switzerland, Belgium, the Netherlands, Luxembourg, the Czech Republic, eastern France, northern Italy, and western

ABOVE: *Throne of Charlemagne at Aachen Cathedral, where Otto was crowned King of Germany in 936.*

Poland. Later, many regions broke away. Though the Holy Roman Emperors continued to rule the German territories (and, to some extent, Italy) until 1806, the empire was reduced to a collection of more-or-less independent states and cities.

The Reformation

The sixteenth century brought a new age to Europe: the Reformation. People started questioning the practices of the Roman Catholic Church. This led to the creation of a new Christian group, the Protestants, or "those who protest."

The movement began in the Germany territories. In 1517, Martin Luther, a German monk, led a revolt against the Church. Lutheranism, the Protestant group founded by Luther, quickly gained a following throughout the country.

ABOVE: Martin Luther (1483–1546), portrait by Lucas Cranach the Elder.

The Reformation sparked an era of unrest in the German territories. German peasants, who lived under miserable conditions, revolted against the lords. Although the peasants' demands were economic and not religious, the Reformation provoked them into launching a full-scale revolt. The rebellion led to the Peasants' War (1524–26), but the peasants were brutally crushed.

The Protestant movement also led to other religious and political divisions, and wars broke out throughout the empire. By 1555, a settlement was struck that recognized Lutheranism as the confession of most of the northern and central German territories. Struggles between Catholics and Protestants, however, did not end with the settlement. Tensions eventually erupted into a series of wars collectively known as the Thirty Years' War (1618–48).

THE GOVERNMENT & HISTORY OF GERMANY

ABOVE: Napoleon Bonaparte *by Jacques Louis David.*

The Peace of Westphalia ended the conflicts, but the German territories remained overwhelmingly divided.

The Deutsches Reich

The German territories had to pay a heavy price for their divided state: France launched a series of aggressions and captured large portions of the region. By 1806, the French general Napoleon Bonaparte dissolved Germany's Holy Roman Empire completely.

The defeat awakened a sense of nationalism in the German territories. They banded together under the Prussian banner (Prussia was the largest German state) and fought the War of Liberation against the French in 1813. The German territories won, and a loose confederation was established.

In 1862, Prussia's prime minister, Otto von Bismarck, took up the cause of German unification. He gathered the German states together to launch successful campaigns against their neighboring states. Encouraged by his success, the German states decided to unite fully. On January 18, 1871, they accepted Prussian King Wilhelm I as their emperor and announced the establishment of the *Deutsches Reich* (the German Empire). With this, Germany the nation-state was born.

EUROPEAN COUNTRIES TODAY: GERMANY

ABOVE: Otto von Bismarck (1815–1898), Chancellor of Germany, known as the Iron Chancellor, c. 1880.

THE GOVERNMENT & HISTORY OF GERMANY

The Deutsches Reich provided for a democratically elected parliament, the Reichstag, but granted it only limited powers. It also gave powers to individual states, though the real authority rested with the Prussian emperor, the *Kaiser*.

World War I and the Weimar Republic

During the period 1871–1910, the Reich fared well, but then the tide turned and things started to sour. A severe economic depression gripped the land. Socialism became a louder voice. The German working class demanded democracy; they wanted the Reichstag to have real powers. Then came World War I, and the situation worsened.

The war started on June 28, 1914, when Gavrilo Princip, a member of the Black Hand, a Serbian nationalist group, assassinated Archduke Ferdinand and his wife, Sophie, of Austria. Russia supported Serbia and Germany supported Austria, so Germany declared war on Russia. After France stepped in on the Russian side, Germany attacked France. Since the quickest route to Paris was through Belgium, German troops invaded that neutral country. Great Britain then declared war on Germany.

At first, German workers supported the war; later, they changed their minds. By 1918, when it became clear that Germany had lost the war, worker protests exploded into a revolution. The emperor went into exile and a new German government, the Weimar Republic, was formed. It asked for peace, but that peace came at a heavy cost. Germany lost both land and money, forcing it to reduce the size of its armed forces.

Nazi Germany and World War II

The large reparations Germany had to make to the war victors placed a great

ABOVE: *Archduke Franz Ferdinand.*

EUROPEAN COUNTRIES TODAY: GERMANY

ABOVE: King Wilhelm I of Prussia, who was later proclaimed German Emperor.

Charlottenburg Palace

Schloss Charlottenburg stands near the edge of Spandau Forest about five miles (8 kilometers) along the Charlottenburger Chaussée from Berlin's Brandenburg Gate. The original building was a country mansion that the elector, and future king, Friedrich III, a ruler more interested in cultural and courtly affairs than mundane administration, built for his wife, Sophie Charlotte, in about 1690. Its first name was Lietzenburg, but when Sophie Charlotte died in the palace in 1705 it was renamed in her memory. The original building was then enlarged on an E-shaped plan around a large courtyard under a Swedish architect, Johann Friedrich Eosander, who is said to have taken advice from the recently appointed imperial architect in Vienna, the great Fischer von Erlach (1656–1723).

The most striking feature of the building is the dome, which surmounts an unusually high, octagonal drum and is topped by an elaborate lantern and large gilded statue of the goddess Fortuna. Many observers have commented critically on the disproportionate height of the dome, which is slightly exaggerated by the wrought-iron railings that, from a distance, mask much of the ground floor of the comparatively modest central block, but this idiosyncrasy has been sanctified by time. The palace was at its most splendid during the reign of Friedrich II (Frederick the Great), who was responsible for its magnificent collection of paintings, including masters of the French rococo such as Boucher and Watteau. Frederick also commissioned the most famous feature of the palace, the Golden Gallery, which was carefully photographed as insurance against war damage in 1943, and destroyed in an air raid less than 24 hours later. Later adornments to the park and gardens include the classical mausoleum by Karl Friedrich Schinkel (1781–1841), and statues of Prussian and German heroes, including a splendid equestrian statue of the Great Elector (father of Friedrich I) by Andreas Schlüter (d. 1714), who, though unsuccessful as an architect, was to Berlin almost what Bernini was to Rome.

Charlottenburg was the final resting place of King Wilhelm I of Prussia. He was buried on March 16, 1888 in the mausoleum in the grounds of the palace.

THE GOVERNMENT & HISTORY OF GERMANY

burden on the country. In 1922–23, the economy collapsed, and the National Socialist German Workers Party, the Nazi Party, attempted a revolution under their leader, Adolf Hitler. The revolution failed. By the late 1920s, the economy seemed to have recovered, and the country again emerged as a cultural and intellectual center.

The worldwide depression of 1929 cut short the good times. The economy was hit badly, and confusion reigned. The Nazi Party grew more powerful, attracting members by offering radical solutions to the country's economic problems and upholding patriotic values.

Unfortunately, most people who supported Hitler had no idea of his real plans. Soon after being appointed as chancellor in 1933, Adolf Hitler became a dictator. Hitler's Germany was unofficially called the Third Reich.

Hitler considered the German people to be superior to all others, and wanted only people of German origin to live in Germany. In 1935, he started a horrifying, inhuman campaign to rid the land of Jews and others who he felt "polluted" the German population. In the following years, the Nazi Party systematically killed millions of people in what they referred to as the "Final Solution."

Hitler also wanted to rebuild the German military might it had lost in World War I. In 1936, he formed an alliance with Italy and signed an anti-Communist agreement with Japan. These three nations became known as the Axis powers.

Hitler's plans for Germany also included getting more land. In 1938,

ABOVE: *In 1934, Hitler became Germany's head of state, with the title of* Führer und Reichskanzler *(Leader and Chancellor of the Reich).*

EUROPEAN COUNTRIES TODAY: GERMANY

Germany occupied Austria, and the next year it seized Czechoslovakia. In August 1939, Germany and the Soviet Union formed a nonaggression pact in which both agreed to remain neutral if the other became involved in a war. Secretly, they also agreed to divide Poland and parts of eastern Europe between them.

On September 1, 1939, Hitler addressed the Reichstag and claimed that Poland had tried to invade Germany. With that, the German military invaded Poland, and the flames of World War II ignited. To defend Poland, Great Britain and France declared war on Germany two days later. Unfortunately, Poland fell to the Germans (who split the country with the Soviets along previously determined lines), who then went on to capture Denmark, Norway, Luxembourg, and Belgium. In May 1940, France too fell into German hands. The Balkans and Crete were the sites of the next German victories.

In June 1941, Hitler reneged on the nonaggression pact and invaded the Soviet Union. At first, the German army met with frightening success, but ultimately the invasion turned out to be a mistake. The massive Soviet Union, its harsh climate, and its scorched-earth policy simply could not be defeated. Having advanced within 30 miles (48.3 kilometers) of Moscow, the German troops were then pushed back. Meanwhile, after Japan's attack on Pearl Harbor on December 7, 1941, the United States entered the conflict. By 1944, Germany was losing the war. Hitler committed suicide on April 30, 1945. A week later, May 7, 1945, the country surrendered. Again, war left Germany in ruins. Rebuilding would be long and hard.

ABOVE: Front page of the US Armed Forces newspaper, The Stars and Stripes, dated May 2, 1945, announcing Hitler's death.

THE GOVERNMENT & HISTORY OF GERMANY

Partition and the Cold War

In July and August 1945, the leaders of Great Britain, the United States, and the Soviet Union decided to rebuild Germany and placed themselves as its governing body. However, the Allies had severe disagreements, and the country was divided into East and West. West Germany, under British and U.S. control, was named the Federal Republic of Germany. Its capital was Bonn. East Germany, under Soviet control, became the German Democratic Republic, and its capital was East Berlin.

West Germany's government was democratic as well as capitalist. It encouraged business, and the economy thrived. East Germany, however, did not fare as well. Ruled by dictators, it was exploited by the Soviet Union. The Soviets stopped almost all trade, communication, and travel between the East and West. The Cold War had begun.

In 1953, strikes and riots broke out in East Germany. Thousands of East Germans fled to West Germany. In August 1961, the Soviets built the Berlin Wall between East and West Berlin to seal off the border. However, protests continued in East Germany.

On November 9, 1989, the East German government, with the approval and encouragement of Mikhail Gorbachev, the reform-minded Soviet leader, finally

German Politics

Germany is a democratic, federal parliamentary republic. Federal legislative power is vested in the Bundestag (the parliament of Germany) and the Bundesrat (the representative body of the *Länder*, Germany's regional states). It is a multiparty system, headed by a chancellor. The current chancellor is Angela Merkel of the Christian Democratic Union.

EUROPEAN COUNTRIES TODAY: GERMANY

ABOVE: A segment of the remains of the Berlin Wall.

opened its borders. The Berlin Wall was breached. East Germany started moving toward a more democratic government.

The Unified Germany of Today

As democracy took root in East Germany, people began considering a unified Germany. East Germany announced its desire for unification in February 1990. In May of that year, East and West Germany signed a treaty for close economic cooperation, and in July the economies of East and West Germany were united.

On October 3, 1990, the unification of the countries was completed. Since East Germany was not prosperous, unification placed a heavy economic burden on West Germany. But the country has struggled past the many challenges it faced.

THE GOVERNMENT & HISTORY OF GERMANY

ABOVE: *The glass dome on top of the Reichstag building in Berlin was designed by the British architect Norman Foster. It was built to symbolize the reunification of Germany in 1990. The building is an important landmark and tourist attraction.*

EUROPEAN COUNTRIES TODAY: GERMANY

Today's Germany is a federation of sixteen states. It is a multiparty democracy. The country's parliament has two houses: the Bundesrat is the upper house and the Bundestag the lower house. Together, the two houses elect their president, who in turn appoints the chancellor, with whom the real power rests.

After two world wars and spending decades divided, Germany has come a long way in its political and economic development. It is now a country of strength and central importance in the European Union. It is also Europe's economic powerhouse.

Text-Dependent Questions

1. When did the Celts inhabit German territory?

2. Who was Gavrilo Princip?

3. Why was the Berlin Wall built?

Research Project

Write an essay on the reunification of Germany, explaining how reunification has affected the country's economy and politics of today.

THE GOVERNMENT & HISTORY OF GERMANY

The Formation of the European Union (EU)

The EU is a confederation of European nations that continues to grow. As of 2017, there are twenty-eight official members. Several other candidates are also waiting for approval. All countries that enter the EU agree to follow common laws about foreign security policies. They also agree to cooperate on legal matters that go on within the EU. The European Council meets to discuss all international matters and make decisions about them. Each country's own concerns and interests are important, though. And apart from legal and financial issues, the EU tries to uphold values such as peace, human dignity, freedom, and equality.

All member countries remain autonomous. This means that they generally keep their own laws and regulations. The idea for a union among European nations was first mentioned after World War II. The war had devastated much of Europe, both physically and financially. In 1950, the French foreign minister suggested that France and West Germany combine their coal and steel industries under one authority. Both countries would have control over the

ABOVE: *The entrance to the European Union Parliament Building in Brussels.*

EUROPEAN COUNTRIES TODAY: GERMANY

Member Countries

Austria	Greece	Romania
Belgium	Hungary	Slovakia
Bulgaria	Ireland	Slovenia
Croatia	Italy	Spain
Cyprus	Latvia	Sweden
Czech Republic	Lithuania	United Kingdom
Denmark	Luxembourg	*(Brexit: For the time*
Estonia	Malta	*being, the United*
Finland	Netherlands	*Kingdom remains a full*
France	Poland	*member of the EU.)*
Germany	Portugal	

industries. This would help them become more financially stable. It would also make war between the countries much more difficult. The idea was interesting to other European countries as well. In 1951, France, West Germany, Belgium, Luxembourg, the Netherlands, and Italy signed the Treaty of Paris, creating the European Coal and Steel Community. These six countries would become the core of the EU.

In 1957, these same countries signed the Treaties of Rome, creating the European Economic Community. In 1965, the Merger Treaty formed the European Community. Finally, in 1992, the Maastricht Treaty was signed. This treaty defined the European Union. It gave a framework for expanding the EU's political role, particularly in the area of foreign and security policy. It would also replace national currencies with the euro. The next year, the treaty went into effect. At that time, the member countries included the original six plus another six who had joined during the 1970s and '80s.

In the following years, the EU would take more steps to form a single market for its members. This would make joining the union even more advantageous. In addition to enlargement, the EU is steadily becoming more integrated through its own policies for closer cooperation between member states.

Words to Understand

eco-friendly: Not environmentally harmful.

exporters: Businesses, persons, or countries that sell to merchants or industrial consumers in foreign countries.

importers: Businesses, persons, or countries that buy from merchants in foreign countries.

BELOW: A vineyard in Palatinate, which is Germany's main wine-growing region. Like many European countries, Germany's wine industry is important to its economy.

Chapter Three
THE GERMAN ECONOMY

Germany is a giant on the world economic stage and overshadows all its European neighbors. Germany has one of the world's most powerful economies, and it is one of the world's largest **importers** and **exporters**. It is also a member of the powerful G8—the eight leading industrial nations in the world.

A Social Market Economy

Germany's success lies in the social market economy structure that it adopted during World War II. A social market economy has both material (financial) and

ABOVE: The Porsche Museum and a Porsche dealership alongside it, Stuttgart. The company is famous for its luxury performance cars that are exported all over the world.

THE GERMAN ECONOMY

social (human) dimensions. The two main aspects of a social market economy are entrepreneurial responsibility and competition. It is an entrepreneur's responsibility to see to her company's growth and to ensure that it can adapt to changing circumstances. The government's role is limited to creating conditions favorable to a healthy economy by contributing to the infrastructure, as well as fair labor and tax laws. The government is also committed to helping those unable to cope with the strenuous demands of a competitive market.

ABOVE: *Tourists at Munich's Oktoberfest (October beer festival).*

EUROPEAN COUNTRIES TODAY: GERMANY

Automotive Industry in Germany

The automotive industry in Germany is one of the largest employers in the country and has a turnover of approximately €404 billion per year. It accounts for around 20 percent of total industry revenue in Germany. Being home to the modern car, the German automobile industry is regarded as the most competitive and innovative in the world. In Europe, Germany accounts for over thirty percent of all passenger cars manufactured (5.75 million) and about 20 percent of all new car registrations (3.35 million). German-designed cars have won many awards, including: European Car of the Year, the International Car of the Year, and the World Car of the Year. The Volkswagen Beetle and Porsche 911 took fourth and fifth places in the Car of the Century award.

Source: VDA 2017

The New Economy

Although one-third of Germany's gross domestic product (GDP) comes from its manufacturing giants, the dominant source of Germany's income today comes from the service sector, which contributes two-thirds of the country's GDP. This includes the country's robust banking industry, the emerging sectors of information technology, and tourism. The dominant force in the German economy is its banking system. Private German banks not only control a substantial stake in German industry but also spread their influence across the globe.

Lufthansa, Germany's national air carrier, carries on its wings another strength of the German economy—tourism. Millions of tourists visit Germany each year. Germany has also built a vibrant trade-fair industry; thousands of visitors use these trade fairs as a gateway into Europe's markets.

45

THE GERMAN ECONOMY

Industry

Heavy industry is still an important part of Germany's economy. Nearly a third of the country's GDP is dependent on the export of machines, motor vehicles, electronics, and chemicals. Supply chains for the steel, coal, cement, and motor vehicle industries are among the most technologically advanced in the world. Germany also has many food and textile enterprises.

The success of Germany's industries is based on the solid infrastructure that Germany has built. The country emphasizes training, both in institutes and the workplace. Research and development is also a major focus area. This has helped Germany engineer world-class products.

The most important branch of Germany's manufacturing sector is the automobile industry. Germany is the third-largest producer of motor vehicles in the world. German-produced vehicles include Volkswagen, BMW, and Porsche. Of the 5,7 million vehicles manufactured in Germany in 2016, approximately two-thirds were exported.

The mechanical engineering, plant construction, and electrical engineering industries have contributed to Germany's solid reputation. Well-known names that form a part of the electronics industry include Siemens, Bosch Group, and AEG.

The German pharmaceutical industry is among the oldest and the best in the world. German medicine makers such as Hoechst, Bayer, and Schering are household names all over the world.

Educational Video

Germany's major chemical manufacturers in the Rhineland.

EUROPEAN COUNTRIES TODAY: GERMANY

ABOVE: *German farming makes up a relatively small proportion of the Germany economy and is heavily subsidized by the EU.*

Agriculture

Despite thousands of acres of open farmland and forests, Germany is predominantly an urban industrial society. Farming brings in only one percent of the GDP and caters mainly to local needs rather than to exports. Agriculture is heavily subsidized by the EU's Common Agricultural Policy and by the German government itself.

Energy Sources and Transportation

Germany is one of the largest energy consumers. Lignite and coal are major domestic sources of energy. Environmental protection and resource conservation are among the most important aims of Germany's EU-driven energy policy, and it has invested heavily in research into various supplies of renewable energy. Geothermal energy sources, solar-power generation,

THE GERMAN ECONOMY

hydroelectricity, as well as biomass research are some of the options being explored. By 2016, almost all of Germany's domestic electricity demand was produced in and **eco-friendly** manner. Germany is home to Europe's largest solar-power plant. Protecting the enviroment is important to Germany and its people.

Transportation

Highways, railways, waterways (both navigable rivers and canals located near modern ports and harbors), and airports make up Germany's complex transportation system. Germany's national airline, Lufthansa, flies around the world and services major international airports.

ABOVE: *A Lufthansa airplane landing at Frankfurt Airport, which is the busiest in Germany.*

EUROPEAN COUNTRIES TODAY: GERMANY

The Economy of Germany

Gross Domestic Product (GDP): US$3.99 trillion (2016 est.)
GDP per Capita: US$48,100 (2016 est.)
Industries: iron, steel, coal, cement, chemicals, machinery, vehicles, machine tools, electronics, food and beverages, shipbuilding, textiles
Agriculture: potatoes, wheat, barley, sugar beet, fruit, cabbages, cattle, pigs, poultry
Export Commodities: machinery, vehicles, chemicals, metals and manufactures, foodstuffs, textiles
Export Partners: US 9.6%, France 8.6%, UK 7.5%, Netherlands 7.5%, China 6%, Italy 4.9%, Austria 4.8%, Poland 4.4%, Switzerland 4.2%
Import Commodities: machinery, vehicles, chemicals, foodstuffs, textiles, metals
Import Partners: Netherlands 13.7%, France 7.6%, China 7.3%, Belgium 6%, Italy 5.2%, Poland 5%, US 4.7%, Czech Republic 4.5%, UK 4.2%, Austria 4.2%, Switzerland 4.2%
Currency: euro (EUR)

Source: www.cia.gov 2017

The Economy Today

Although Germany's economy is affluent and technologically advanced, the country has experieced slowdowns in the past. Internal and external economic problems slowed the growth rate to less than one percent in 2003–4. This slowdown stemmed from two dominant sources. The first was the unification of West Germany with East Germany, which has cost taxpayers billions of euros.

The second reason for the country's sluggish economic growth was unemployment and the cost of the country's welfare bill. Germany had one of

THE GERMAN ECONOMY

the highest unemployment rates in Europe. According to 2004 estimates, more than 10 percent of the population was without a job. With one in ten people unemployed, consumer spending was low, forcing German manufacturers to focus on international markets for their growth. Unemployment and an aging population pushed social security payments to a level exceeding contributions from workers.

However, since then, the German economy has improved, helped by the steady fall in the value of the euro, the currency adopted by many nations in the EU. A weaker euro is good news because it means that German products become cheaper and therefore more desirable for the rest of the world.

Getting Back on Its Feet

Germany found its way out of recession by making swift economic reforms after implementing an ambitions recovery plan. The country was well into economic recovery by the end of 2009. Growth continued through to 2012 at a rate higher than its local neighboring nations, and by 2014 Germany recorded the highest trade surplus in the world.

Today, Germany's economy is made up largely the service sector, approximately a third of its revenue is attributed to industry, with a smaller percentage of its economy in agriculture. Germany's national output derives from exporting manufactured goods, including vehicles, machinery, chemical goods, electronic products, electrical equipment, pharmaceuticals, transport equipment, metal, food products, rubber, and plastics.

Germany has been growing solidly in recent years, driven largely by private consumption. The economy has experienced a few bumps in the road, but overall it appears to still be relatively secure. Consumer confidence is currently high, and the German government has allocated billions of euros for infrastructure improvements and investment through 2018. Low international oil prices and a strong labor market with higher wages bode well for domestic consumption, while exports have increased on the back of a weak euro. As a result, the German economy is expected to grow further.

EUROPEAN COUNTRIES TODAY: GERMANY

ABOVE: The Ruhr is a heavily industrialized region in western Germany.

Text-Dependent Questions

1. How important is manufacturing to Germany?

2. Why are low oil prices good for the German economy?

3. Why does Germany benefit from a weak euro?

Research Project

Which countries are members of the G8 and how often do they gather? Why do they meet and what do they discuss?

Words to Understand

Balkan: A geographic area in eastern and southeastern Europe.

compulsory: Required by or as if by law.

secular: Not related to religious matters.

RIGHT: St. John's Church (Johanneskirche) in Stuttgart. This Protestant church dates from 1876 and is an example of the Gothic Revival style.

Chapter Four
CITIZENS OF GERMANY: PEOPLE, CUSTOMS & CULTURE

Germany, home to over 82 million people, is the second most populated country in Europe. Most Germans are of northern and central European descent. Many can trace their ancestry to ancient tribes such as the Cimbri, Franks, Goths, and Teutons. The country's official language is German.

Non-German-speaking minorities make up a small proportion of Germany's population. Native, non-German-speaking groups such as Danes, Frisians, Roma (often called Gypsies), and Sorbs/Wends make up part of this population. Immigrants, such as "guest workers," from Turkey, Italy, and the Balkan countries make up another portion of the non-German-speaking population.

Religion
The German people have full freedom to choose their faith and religion. While 70 percent of the population belong to Christian religions, Islam and Judaism are also practiced. Protestantism is most popular in the north. Roman Catholicism is more prevalent in the south and west. About half the population in what was formerly East Germany has no religious affiliation.

Education and Sports
Germans take both education and sports very seriously. Almost all adults can read and write, and most can speak at least one foreign language. Nearly half the population plays some form of sport. The country produces great academicians and famous sports figures.

German education is compulsory and job oriented. Every child between the ages of six and sixteen must attend school. The school system, though, is quite different from most in North America. To begin, all children attend *Grundschule*, elementary school, until the fourth grade. Then the students are

CITIZENS OF GERMANY: PEOPLE, CUSTOMS & CULTURE

ABOVE: *Young school children participating in a music lesson in a school in Frankfurt.*

divided into three different school streams. Some children go to *Hauptschule*, a job-oriented type of school that concentrates on teaching practical skills. Other young people attend *Realschule*, which offers a broader general education. And nearly half the children enroll in the *Gymnasium*, the academic, college-preparatory school. Germany has about sixty universities and many technical and specialized colleges. It has produced great scientists such as Albert Einstein, Max Planck, and Otto Hahn.

When it comes to sports, Germans don't believe in just watching games. They go out and play the games themselves. Soccer is by far the most popular sport. Germany has won the World Cup three times. Tennis, hockey, and basketball also have fans. Bicycling, canoeing, rowing, sailing, swimming, skiing, and hiking are other popular sports.

EUROPEAN COUNTRIES TODAY: GERMANY

Educational Video

A video about Germany's complicated education system.

ABOVE: Nico Rosberg was Formula One World Champion in 2016, with the hugely successful Mercedes team. He announced his retirement in 2017, but remains an ambassador for Mercedes.

55

CITIZENS OF GERMANY: PEOPLE, CUSTOMS & CULTURE

Food and Drink

Known for their robust appetites, Germans have traditionally preferred simple, substantial fare. *Frühstück*, the classic German breakfast, consists of breads, rolls, jam, and honey served with coffee and milk. *Mittagessen*, lunch, the main meal of the day, usually consists of meat, potatoes, and vegetables. *Abendbrot*, supper, is generally a cold meal, eaten early. Many Germans often brighten up their afternoons with *kaffe und kuchen*—coffee and cakes.

Modern lifestyles have brought some changes in eating habits. Germans are cutting back on meat. They enjoy foreign foods such as pizza, pasta, and doner kebabs (a lamb dish). Yet, even today, the old favorites—meat, potatoes, sausages, pickles, bread, and cakes—dominate German cuisine.

Wurst (sausage) and *Aufschnitt* (cold cuts) are the most distinctive foods associated with Germany. About 1,500 varieties are available. An assortment of breads, most made from rye, and rich cakes mark German baking.

As for beverages, most Germans prefer coffee to tea. Beer is the most popular alcoholic drink, followed by wine.

ABOVE: *This typical German dish is pork hock with sauerkraut (fermented cabbage).*

EUROPEAN COUNTRIES TODAY: GERMANY

Bratkartoffeln (Fried Potatoes)

Serves 4

Ingredients
2 lbs peeled and cooked potatoes
1 tbs of fennel seeds
3 tbs cooking oil
Salt and pepper
1 finely sliced red onion
sprig of rosemary

Directions
Cut the potatoes into even thick slices. Heat the oil over a medium-high heat. Add the onion and fennel seeds, and fry until they are soft. Add the potatoes to the pan, stir once and place them so each piece is touching the bottom. Cook for 3 to 5 minutes until they are golden brown. Then turn them over and repeat on the other side. Add a litle more oil if necessary. Season with salt and pepper and garnish with a sprig of rosemary.

Springerle (Cookies)
These are an embossed cookie. A mould is used to emboss designs on the dough.

Makes approx. 30 cookies

Ingredients
4 eggs
30g (1 oz) butter
2 tsp baking powder
¼ tsp salt
400g (14 oz) caster sugar
500g (1 1/8 lb) plain flour
4 tbs aniseseed

Directions
Beat eggs in large mixing bowl until very light. Add sugar and butter. Cream together until light and fluffy. Sieve flour, baking powder, and salt. Add dry ingredients and combine. Knead dough until smooth. Cover dough and allow to chill in refrigerator for at least 2 hours. Roll onto slightly floured board to 1cm (¼ in.) thickness. Then roll again with springerle roller to make designs. Cut at border. Sprinkle aniseseed on clean tea towel and place cookies on it. Allow to stand overnight (don't cover) to dry. Bake 12 to 15 minutes at 160°C/320°F Allow to cool.

CITIZENS OF GERMANY: PEOPLE, CUSTOMS & CULTURE

ABOVE: Opening parade of the Oktoberfest (October beer festival) in Munich.

Festivals and Events

Germans really know how to celebrate a holiday. Parades, fancy dress parties, crowds on the streets, floats, shows, and dances—Germany puts on a grand spectacle to mark its festivals and events.

While the country only observes nine religious and two **secular** holidays nationwide, many festivals and events are celebrated on a regional or even town-specific scale. Many of these holidays are nonreligious. Berlin, for instance, is famous for its film festival. Munich hosts *Oktoberfest*, an annual sixteen-day celebration of beer. *Schultüte* is a festival for children. Children are given a paper cone full of candy, pencils, and other small gifts which is also called a *Schultüte* on their first day of first grade.

EUROPEAN COUNTRIES TODAY: GERMANY

Music and Literature

Having produced numerous great poets, thinkers, and musical virtuosos, Germany can truly be called a land of genius.

In literature, the first widely recognized German work was Martin Luther's sixteenth-century translation of the Bible. The greatest period for German literature lasted from about 1750 to 1830. Greats such as Johann Wolfgang von Goethe, Friedrich Schiller, and Friedrich Hölderlin were the leading authors of this period. Later German writers Thomas Mann, Hermann Hesse, Heinrich Böll, and Günter Grass have all received the Nobel Prize for Literature.

Germany enjoys a special place in children's literature. The Grimm Brothers traveled the German countryside, recording what have become some of the world's best-loved fairy-tales. Characters such as Hansel and Gretel, the Pied Piper of Hamelin, and Cinderella were all based on German folktales.

Johann Sebastian Bach established the great tradition of German music in the early 1700s. Ludwig van Beethoven was the virtuoso of the 1800s. Felix Mendelssohn, Franz Schubert, Robert Schumann, Richard Wagner, Richard Strauss, Arnold Schoenburg, and Kurt Weill, all great composers, carried the baton through to the twentieth century. Works by these classical composers continue to be enjoyed the world over. However, Germans today enjoy a wide variety of music, including hip-hop, rock, and pop.

ABOVE: *Friedrich Schiller.*

ABOVE: *Johann Sebastian Bach.*

ABOVE: *Thomas Mann.*

The Bauhaus, Dessau

The Bauhaus was designed by German architect Walter Gropius (1883–1969). Gropius was a former student of Peter Behrens, an advocate of mass production in housing, and one of the originators of the International Modern style exemplified in cubic blocks, glass walls, no extraneous decoration, asymmetrical composition, and little colour other than white. The Bauhaus "Building House," as Gropius renamed it, was an arts school that aimed to encourage all kinds of artists to work together to "build the future." Perhaps his greatest achievement was to make a potentially difficult group of the finest contemporary artists and designers cooperate so successfully.

The Bauhaus was originally dominated by Expressionism and the Arts and Crafts tradition, but soon became oriented more toward technology and industry. It became the heart of the International Modern movement, and when it moved to Dessau in 1925–26, after its left-leanings had prompted the Weimar government to withhold funds, Gropius designed new buildings that were intended to represent the "new unity" of art and technology, as proclaimed by Gropius in a 1924 memorandum. The complex comprised the impressive main building with its huge glass walls, and several other buildings, including a two-storey structure that bridged a street and housed Gropius's office and homes for teachers. The students' (originally called "apprentices") block included a gymnasium as well as classrooms, a dining hall, and living accommodation. There was also a theater. Function is the guide to form, and the buildings, which have recently been restored, are no less visually impressive for being well-adapted to practical purposes.

Gropius resigned from the school in 1928 and was eventually succeeded by Ludwig Mies van der Rohe. As had happened during the Weimar period, the school fell from political favor and was shut down in 1932. Mies restarted it on a private basis in Berlin, but when the Nazis gained power in 1933, they closed it for good. In a way, this was the making of the Bauhaus, because its staff and ideas were scattered abroad, to the USA in particular, and its influence thus greatly expanded.

CITIZENS OF GERMANY: PEOPLE, CUSTOMS & CULTURE

ABOVE: Praying Woman, *1892 by Käthe Kollwitz.*

EUROPEAN COUNTRIES TODAY: GERMANY

Arts and Architecture

Germany's artists rank among the most innovative in Europe in terms of architecture, design, sculpture, painting, and printmaking. Huge fortress-like cathedrals, tall churches crowned with pointed arches, and ornate castles decorated with dramatic oil paintings and frescoes dot the countryside.

Historically, Germany has not only been a leader in architecture; it's also been a leader in painting. Germany gave birth to the Expressionist style of painting. George Grosz and Käthe Kollwitz are well-known Expressionist artists. Arising in the early twentieth century, the Expressionist movement sought to express emotions by distorting and exaggerating natural forms.

Today, modern mediums such as photography, video art, metal sculpture, environment-driven art, film, and fashion photography flourish in Germany.

Text-Dependent Questions

1. What kinds of foods do Germans like to eat?

2. Who was Richard Strauss?

3. Who was Walter Gropius?

Research Project

Germany is well known for its talented composers of music. Write an essay about the life and works of Ludwig van Beethoven.

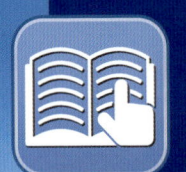

Words to Understand

media: The means of communication that reach large numbers of people, such as television, newspapers, and radio.

Oktoberfest: a fall festival usually featuring beer drinking.

urban: Relating to, or constituting, a city.

BELOW: Aerial view of the Berlin skyline and Spree River. Berlin Cathedral (Berliner Dom) is on the left.

Chapter Five
THE FAMOUS CITIES OF GERMANY

Today's Germany is an extremely **urban** society. Over 80 percent of its population live in cities and towns. Most Germans earn a fairly comfortable income and lead prosperous lifestyles. Urban German families tend to be quite small; German couples usually have only one child, and many have none at all.

Most of Germany's cities are medium-sized or small; only a few large cities exist. A majority of German cities were founded centuries ago. Today, they offer their residents every modern convenience yet maintain their medieval character. Castles, stately timbered homes, cathedrals, abbeys, romantic winding streets, and even Roman ruins merge with modern structures to give German towns a unique identity that blends old and new.

German cities also consciously promote a rich cultural life. Many towns subsidize theater, opera, music festivals, and galleries.

Germany is comprised of sixteen states (*Länder*) whose population densities vary greatly. The most densely populated are urban states like Berlin, Hamburg, and Bremen. The least densely populated are Mecklenburg-West Pomerania and Brandenburg, both mostly rural. The state with the largest population, one-fifth of the

ABOVE: *The famous TV Tower at Alexanderplatz, Berlin.*

THE FAMOUS CITIES OF GERMANY

Educational Video

Top attractions and things to do in Berlin.

ABOVE: *Berlin Cathedral (Berliner Dom) is situated on Museum Island in the Mitte district. It was completed in 1905 and is Berlin's largest church, and one of the major sights in the city's center.*

EUROPEAN COUNTRIES TODAY: GERMANY

ABOVE: *The Brandenburg Gate is an eighteenth-century neoclassical monument in Berlin, built on the orders of King Friedrich Wilhelm II of Prussia.*

nation's total, is North Rhine-Westphalia. This state has many industrial cities. The largest state, Bavaria, has a low population density. Its capital, Munich, however, is a crowded urban center.

Berlin

Berlin is Germany's capital and most populated city. After World War II, the Berlin Wall divided it into two cities, East Berlin and West Berlin. Today, reunited Berlin is an acknowledged seat of culture. It hosts events such as the Jazz Festival and the International Film Festival. It is home to more than 170 museums, including Europe's largest museum complex, Museum Island. Berlin also boasts extensive woodlands and rivers that meander through the city. At the center of the city lies the popular Tiergarten park.

THE FAMOUS CITIES OF GERMANY

Hamburg

Germany's second most populated city, Hamburg, is one of the richest metropolises in Europe. Its wealth is a result of its thriving harbor and powerful media industry. A grid of narrow canals and three rivers—the Elbe, Alster, and Bille—shapes the city's port. Each year, about 12,000 ships move some 70 million tons of goods, making Hamburg the most important port in Germany and one of the largest harbors in Europe. Because of its coastal location, Hamburg has also attracted immigrants from all over Europe, who make up 15 to 20 percent of its population.

ABOVE: *The Speicherstadt, or warehouse district, in Hamburg was designated a UNESCO World Hertitage Site in 2015.*

EUROPEAN COUNTRIES TODAY: GERMANY

ABOVE: *The town hall in Hamburg's city center was built close to the Alster River.*

THE FAMOUS CITIES OF GERMANY

Munich

Situated in the southern state of Bavaria, Munich is one of Germany's leading industrial cities and the headquarters of world famous car manufacturer BMW (Bayerische Motoren Werke [Bavarian Motor Works]). The city is proud of its many museums and splendid architecture.

Munich's **Oktoberfest** is hailed as the world's largest fair. Also called the Wiesn, the Oktoberfest is an annual celebration of beer. People from all over the world come to enjoy sausages and sample the beverages on tap in the many beer tents. The good times last for sixteen days.

ABOVE: *The rooftops of Munich's old town. The city is proud of its splendid architecture.*

EUROPEAN COUNTRIES TODAY: GERMANY

ABOVE: Marienplatz is the central square in Munich. Its main feature is the impressive town hall. It has been the city's main square since 1158.

71

THE FAMOUS CITIES OF GERMANY

Nymphenburg, Munich

The "Castle of the Nymphs" on the outskirts of Munich was the summer palace of the rulers and later kings of Bavaria. It is essentially a collection of buildings in which some parts are of greater interest than others. The original building, the five-floor central block, was built in 1664 by the Bolognese architect, Agostino Barelli, who introduced the Italian baroque to southern Germany. The matching blocks on either side, linked by arcaded galleries, were built in the next reign, and the famous gardens were laid out in 1701 by Carbonet, a former pupil of Le Nôtre at Versailles. At about the same time, the original interior was reconstructed to accommodate a great hall three storeys high, for which the arched windows in the facade were installed. The addition of two further buildings on the wings in the mid-eighteenth century, almost matching their neighbours, completed the scheme.

EUROPEAN COUNTRIES TODAY: GERMANY

ABOVE: The BMW Building and Museum are located near the Olympic Village in Munich. The buildings were finished in 1972, shortly before the Summer Olympics. The tower's exterior is supposed to mimic the shape of four cylinders in a car's engine. The museum represents a cylinder head. Both buildings were designed by the Austrian architect, Karl Schwanzer.

🇩🇪 **THE FAMOUS CITIES OF GERMANY**

The Rhine-Ruhr Area

Crowded urban centers have also developed in industrial areas. The Rhine-Ruhr area, the center of German heavy industry, is a vast population hub. Five large cities—Düsseldorf, Duisburg, Dortmund, Essen, and Cologne—make up the Ruhr area. Many people live in adjacent areas or towns and commute to the cities, so these urban centers service far more people than those living within the city limits.

ABOVE: *Cologne Cathedral and the Hohenzollern Bridge that crosses the Rhine.*

EUROPEAN COUNTRIES TODAY: GERMANY

ABOVE: Düsseldorf is an impressive modern city with innovative architecture, lively nightlife and an art scene to rival many higher-profile cities. It is an important center for business such as banking, advertising, fashion, and telecommunications, which have made it one of Germany's wealthiest cities.

THE FAMOUS CITIES OF GERMANY

Bremen

Though Hamburg is Germany's largest harbor city, Bremen is the most important economically. It houses one of the world's most modern container terminals and handles nearly 1.3 million crates annually. The German Maritime Museum, with its collection of five hundred ship models, is a favorite site for visitors to Bremen. Germany's ever-increasing aerospace industry also has a strong base in Bremen.

ABOVE: *The Weser River and the Lutheran St. Martin's Church in the old town of Bremen.*

EUROPEAN COUNTRIES TODAY: GERMANY

ABOVE: *A bronze statue by Gerhard Marcks, depicting the "Town Musicians of Bremen" from a fairytale by the Brothers Grimm. The statue was erected in 1953. Note the front hooves that have become shiny. Touching the front hooves is said to make wishes come true.*

THE FAMOUS CITIES OF GERMANY

Xanten and Lindau

One of Germany's oldest towns, Xanten dates back to around 100 CE. One of the biggest Roman settlements was located here. Today, this town of picturesque medieval streets, all built around thousand-year-old St. Viktor's Cathedral, combines cosmopolitan flair with an easygoing country attitude.

Lindau is a holiday town. Located on an island in Lake Constance, where Germany, Austria, and Switzerland meet, Lindau offers a spectacular view of the Alps and has a carefully preserved medieval town center. Cities like these make Germany a unique and valuable member of the European Union.

ABOVE: *Attractions in Xanten include the medieval town center, the cathedral, and many museums.*

EUROPEAN COUNTRIES TODAY: GERMANY

Archaeological Park & Roman Museum

The Xanten Archaeological Park, one of the largest archaeological open air museums in the world, houses the remains of the Roman settlement of *Colonia Ulpia Traiana*.

In the park, some buildings have been partly reconstructed, others rebuilt and furnished to give visitors an idea of what the settlement would have been like. Original remains of Roman buildings can also be seen.

The exhibition features a chronological tour of Xanten's eventful Roman history with over 2,500 exhibits and the latest museum technology to create a vivid picture of the daily life of the Romans in Germania. Overall, Xanten Archaeological Park offers a fascinating insight into life in this Roman settlement and really lets you immerse yourself in its history. You can even dress up like a Roman.

THE FAMOUS CITIES OF GERMANY

ABOVE: Lindau is a large town and an island on Bodensee (Lake Constance), Bavaria.

EUROPEAN COUNTRIES TODAY: GERMANY

ABOVE: The Mangturm Tower and several hotels and restaurants in the harbor of Lindau Island.

Text-Dependent Questions

1. Which city is the capital of Bavaria?

2. What is Germany's second most populated city?

3. Where is the German Maritime Museum?

Research Project

Draw a map of Germany showing each state and its capital city.

Words to Understand

assertive: Confident in behavior, manner, or style.

dedication: A feeling of very strong support for or loyalty to someone or something.

democracy: A form of government in which people choose leaders by voting.

BELOW: *Frankfurt am Main is in central Germany on the river Main. It is a major financial hub that is home to the European Central Bank.*

Chapter Six
A BRIGHT FUTURE FOR GERMANY

Since World War II, Germany has come along way. Much of its success has been the result of the hardworking and industrious German population. This **dedication** and devotion to hard work has often given the Germans an image of being reserved and **assertive**, however, this is far from true. Germans are very good-natured, friendly, and neighborly. When visting Germany, foreigners are often very surprised how easygoing the Germans are. Germans place high importance on leisure and culture, and enjoy the benefits of life in a liberal **democracy** that has become ever more integrated with and central to a united Europe.

Living Standards

In the western part of Germany, the standard of living is among the highest in the world. The distribution of wealth compares favorably with that of other advanced countries. eastern Germany lags behind the west, but is catching up. Germans are known for being savers and they rarely use credit facilities. Incentives to save are offered by the state, not only in the form of housing subsidies and tax

ABOVE: *EU and German flags.*

83

A BRIGHT FUTURE FOR GERMANY

concessions but also through bonus saving schemes. For those on lower incomes, savings of up to a fixed amount kept in a bank or savings institution for seven years are granted a generous bonus by the government. The government encourages the accumulation of capital assets whereby workers can agree to pay into a longer-term savings plan, such as a home-savings contract, or are given a "worker savings grant" by the state.

Fortunately, for German workers, there is a relatively small gap between the earnings of blue-collar workers and white-collar workers; however, top management is generously rewarded in income and benefits. As in most EU countries, value-added tax means that low- and medium-income workers collectively bear a greater relative tax burden. Germany's unemployment rate, and is currently 6.2 percent which is has come down in recent years.

ABOVE: *German shoppers in the city of Essen, North Rhine-Westphalia. Germans have a high standard of living and good spending power.*

EUROPEAN COUNTRIES TODAY: GERMANY

ABOVE: Photovoltaic, wind, and other forms of renewable power are very important to Germany. Renewables account for almost all of the country's domestic power.

Power and Renewable Energy

German government policy has set a dual goal to move from fossil fuel-based energy generation to a largely carbon-free energy sector, and at the same time phasing out nuclear energy by 2022. While some other nations have viewed this policy as a panic reaction following the Fukushima disaster in 2011, this new policy has actually had a long history and is deeply rooted in German society. Antinuclear movements started in Germany in the 1970s when local initiatives organized protests against plans to build nuclear power stations. In 1986, large parts of Germany were contaminated with radioactive material following the Chernobyl disaster in the Ukraine.

Germany now boasts that it is the world's first major renewable energy economy, with renewables supplying nearly all of domestic electricity. Germany's federal government is developing new technologies for increasing renewable energy sources, with a particular focus on offshore wind farms.

A BRIGHT FUTURE FOR GERMANY

A major challenge is the development of that infrastructure which can transmit the power generated in the North Sea to the large industrial consumers in the south of the country.

Cultural institutions

Germany has always supported the country's cultural, educational, and scientific resources. Nearly all of its important organizations are maintained entirely or in part by public funds. The country is devoted to promoting and protecting the culture, life, and language of the German peoples and familiarizing the German public with the culture and life of other nations around the world. As well as nurturing and protecting its own culture, Germany also

ABOVE: The U-Tower is a former brewery building in the city of Dortmund. it is now a center for the arts and creativity, and houses the Museum Ostwall.

EUROPEAN COUNTRIES TODAY: GERMANY

ABOVE: *Neue Nationalgalerie in Berlin is a masterpiece of modern architecture designed by Mies van der Rohe in 1968. It is dedicated to modern art.*

fosters the advancement of cultural and educational ties with the world's less-developed countries. Not only has Germany played a major role in the exporting of technological skill and capital for developing resources, but it also has become a major center for the education and training of students from these countries in the all the major professions.

Germany's Goethe-Institut Inter Nationes (formerly the Goethe Institut of Munich) was founded in 1951. It has some 140 branches in more than 70 countries. It has founded schools in Germany and overseas that offer instruction in the German language. It also maintains lending libraries and audiovisual centers, and sponsors exhibits, film programs, musical, and theatrical events, and lectures by important and eminent individuals.

A BRIGHT FUTURE FOR GERMANY

Angela Merkel

Angela Dorothea Merkel is a German politician and has been the chancellor of Germany since 2005. She has also been the leader of the center-right Christian Democratic Union since 2000. In September 2017 she was voted in for a fourth term. However, she won with less of a majority than in previous elections. Votes were lost to right-wing parties. This was considered to be a backlash against immigration into the country.

Germany's Future

Germany is one of the world's leading economies and is considered to be the powerhouse of the European Union. Its economy will be improved further by European integration and the adoption of the euro by other countries. Despite the challeges of the integration and upgrading of the East German economy, the restructuring of its economic sectors, and its aging population, Germany has continued to grow. Germany has always had special interest in promoting EU enlargement by the accession of Eastern European countries. However, this enlargement has also prompted concerns about the influx of immigrants and the high financial costs posed by new countries joining the EU. An important priority of the federal government is fostering the development and growth of eastern Germany, a major burden on the federal budget throughout the 1990s. Germany's responsibility as an influential member of the

EUROPEAN COUNTRIES TODAY: GERMANY

international community will also grow in areas such as economic assistance for developing countries, environmental protection, and cooperation in combating corruption and transnational organized crime. While there is no doubt of Germany's success economically, its future is dependent on the stability of the world around it, for as an exporting nation, it requires a good marketplace for its goods. The country will also depend on a successful European monetary policy.

Text-Dependent Questions

1. Why is the west of Germany more prosperous than the east?

2. Why are the Germans so good at saving their money?

3. Why is Germany closing its nuclear power stations?

Research Project

Write an essay on renewable energy in Germany and investigate how successful the country is at achieving its goals.

CHRONOLOGY

1000 BCE	Tribes from northern Europe take over large portions of the land that is now Germany.
800 CE	Charlemagne's empire is established.
962	Otto I is crowned emperor and establishes the Holy Roman Empire.
1517	The Reformation begins in Germany.
1618	A protest by Bohemian Protestants in Prague marks the beginning of the Thirty Years' War.
1792	The war against revolutionary France begins.
1813–15	Liberation wars against Napoleonic France begin.
1815	The Holy Alliance between Russia, Austria, and Prussia is founded to suppress liberal movements.
1870–71	The Franco-German War is waged.
1871	The German Empire is founded with Bismarck as chancellor. Emperor Wilhelm I is crowned in Versailles.
1914	World War I begins.
1918	Germany is defeated in World War I.
1919	A German national assembly is elected to write a constitution, and the Weimar Republic is established.
1933	Adolf Hitler is appointed chancellor.
1939	Germany invades Poland, and World War II begins.
1945	The Allies defeat Germany and divide it into East and West.
1957	The European Economic Community begins between Germany, France, Belgium, Italy, Luxembourg, and the Netherlands.
1990	East and West Germany unify and become a single entity again.
1997	Germany signs the new EU Treaty, the Treaty of Amsterdam.
2002	Euro notes and coins replace the deutsche mark.
2005	Christian Democrat leader Angela Merkel becomes chancellor.
2011	Chancellor Merkel defends her decision to back a second huge bailout for Greece.
2014	Germany adopts a minimum wage for the first time, setting it at € 8.50 an hour.
2016	Attacks by migrant Islamic State sympathisers in Wüerzburg and Ansbach leave seventeen people injured.
2017	Chancellor Merkel is elected for a fourth term in September.

FURTHER READING & INTERNET RESOURCES

Further Reading

Egert-Romanowska, Joanna. Omilanowska, Malgorzata. *DK Eyewitness Travel Guide: Germany*. London: DK, 2016.

McCormick, John. *Understanding the European Union: A Concise Introduction*. London: Palgrave Macmillan, 2017.

Mason, David S. *A Concise History of Modern Europe: Liberty, Equality, Solidarity*. London: Rowman & Littlefield, 2015.

Steves, Rick. *Rick Steves Germany*. Edmonds: Rick Steves' Europe, Inc., 2018.

Internet Resources

Germany Travel Information and Travel Guide
www.lonelyplanet.com/germany

German Tourism Guide
http://www.germany.travel/en/index.html?

Germany: Country Profile
http://www.bbc.com/news/world-europe-17299607

Germany: CIA World Factbook
https://www.cia.gov/library/publications/the-world-factbook/geos/gm.html

The Official Website of the European Union
europa.eu/index_en.htm

Publisher's note:
The websites listed on this page were active at the time of publication. The publisher is not responsible for websites that have changed their addressees or discontinued operation since the date of publication. The publisher will review and update the website list upon each reprint.

INDEX

A
Aachen Cathedral, 26
Adder, 21
AEG, 46
Agriculture, 47, 49
Allies, 36
Alps, 8, 16, 17, 21
Alster river, 69
Ancient Germany, 23
Animals, 18, 19–21
Architecture, 63
Art, 63
Artifacts, 23
Arts and Crafts tradition, 60
Assassination, 30
Aufschnitt, 56
Austria, 7, 11, 14, 26, 30, 49, 78
    occupation of, 35
Automotive industry, 45, 46
Axis powers, 34

B
Bach, Johann Sebastian, 59
Baden-Baden, 14
Baden-Württemberg, 8, 10, 14
Balkans, 35, 53
Baltic Sea, 7, 8, 11
Banking, 45
Barelli, Agostino, 72
Bauhaus, 60–61
Bavaria, 14, 22, 67, 70, 72, 80
Bavarian
    Alps, 12, 14
    Forest, 20
    National Park, 18
Bayer, 46
Beer, 56, 70
Beethoven, Ludwig van, 59
Behrens, Peter, 60
Belgium, 7, 11, 26, 30, 40, 49
    invasion of, 30
    and World War II, 35
Berlin, 32, 38, 57, 61, 64, 65, 67, 87
    Cathedral (Berliner Dom), 64, 66
    International Film Festival, 57, 67
    Jazz Festival, 67
    Wall, 36–37, 67
Bible, 59
Bingen, 15
Birds, 21
Birth rate, 9
Bismarck, Otto von, 28, 29
Black Forest, 10, 12, 14
BMW, 46, 70
    Building and Museum, 73
Bodensee. *See* Lake Constance
Böll, Heinrich, 59
Bonaparte, Napoleon, 28
Bonn, 36
Borders, 7, 23
Bosch Group, 46
Boucher, 32
Brandenburg, 65
    Gate, 32, 67
Bratkartoffein, 57
Bremen, 65, 76
Brothers Grimm, 77
Brussels, 40
Bundesrat, 36, 39
Bundestag, 36, 39

C
Capital, 67
Capitalism, 36
Carbonet, 72
Celts, 23
Chancellor, 36, 88
Charlemagne, 24
    Throne of, 26
Charlemagne (Dürer), 24
Charlottenburg
    Chaussée, 32
    Palace, 32–33
Chernobyl disaster, 85
Chocolate-cherry cake, 14
Christian Democratic Union, 36, 88
Christianity, 26, 53
Cinderella, 59
Cities, 65–82
Climate, 7, 17
Coal, 47
Coffee and cakes, 56
Cold cuts, 56
Cold War, 36–37
Cologne, 74
    Cathedral, 74
Cookies, 57
Cultivation, 11
Cultural region, 23
Currency, 49
Czechoslovakia, 35
Czech Republic, 7, 11, 26, 49

D
Danes, 53
Danube river, 14, 16
David, Jacques Louis, 28
Death rate, 9
Democracy, 30, 36
Denmark, 7, 35
Depression, 30
Deutsches Reich, 28–30
Dortmund, 74, 86
Duisburg, 74
Düsseldorf, 74, 75

E
East Berlin, 36
East Germany, 8, 36, 37, 49, 53
    economy, 88
Economy, 43–50
    collapse, 34
    current, 49–50
    depression, 34
    new, 45
    recession, 50
    renewable energy, 85
    social market, 43–44
Education, 53–54, 87
Einstein, Albert, 54
Elbe river, 16
Elections, 88

92

INDEX

Elevation, 7
Emperor, 28, 31
Ems river, 16
Energy, 47–48, 85–86
   biomass, 48
   geothermal, 47
   hydroelectricity, 48
   nuclear, 85
   photovoltaic, 85
   renewable, 85
   solar, 47
   wind, 85
Environment, protection of, 47
Eosander, Johann Friedrich, 32
Essen, 74, 84
Eurasian
   lynx, 20, 21
   otter, 21
   wolf, 18
Euro, 49, 50, 88
European
   badger, 19
   Car of the Year, 45
   Central Bank, 82
   Coal and Steel Community, 40
   Community, 40
   Economic Community, 40
   Parliament Building, 40
European Union (EU), 23, 39, 88
   autonomy, 40
   Common Agriculture Policy, 47
   enlargement, 88
   flag, 83
   formation, 40–41
   members, 40, 41
   values, 40
Exports, 46, 49
Expressionism, 60, 63

F

Farming, 12, 47
Federal Republic of Germany, 8, 23, 36
Federation, 39
Feldberg, 14
Ferdinand, Archduke Franz, 30
Fertility rate, 9
Festivals, 57
Feudal system, 26
"Final Solution," 34
First German Reich, 24
Fish, 21
Flag, 8, 83
Flooding, 7
Food and drink, 56–57
Forests, 19. *See also* Black Forest
Formula One World Champion, 55
Fortuna, 32
Foster, Norman, 38
France, 7, 11, 14, 24, 26, 28, 30, 40, 49
   and World War II, 35
Frankfurt
   Airport, 48
   am Main, 82
Franks, 24
Friederich
   II, 33
   III, 32
Frisians, 53
Frühstück, 56
Führer und Reichskanzler, 34. *See also* Hitler, Adolph
Fukushima disaster, 85
Future, 83–89

G

G8, 43
Geography, 7, 11–21
German
   language, 9
   Maritime Museum, 76
German Democratic Republic, 36
Germani, 23
Goethe, Johann Wolfgang von, 59
Goethe-Institut Inter Nationes, 87
Golden Gallery, 32
Gorbachev, Mikhail, 36–37
Gothic Revival style, 53
Government, 23–41
Grass, Günter, 59
Great Britain, 30, 36
   and World War II, 35
Great Elector, 32
Grimm Brothers, 59
Gropius, Walter, 60
Gross domestic product (GDP), 45, 47, 49
   per capita, 49
Grosz, George, 63
Grundschule, 53
Gymnasium, 54

H

Hahn, Otto, 54
Hamburg, 65, 68–69
Hansel and Gretel, 59
Harz
   Mountains, 12, 20
   National Park, 20
Hauptschule, 54
Heidelberg, 8
Hesse, Herman, 59
Highlands, 12
History, 23–41
Hitler, Adolph, 34
   chancellor, 34
   death of, 35
   dictator, 34
Hoechst, 46
Hohenschwangau, 22
Hohenzollern Bridge, 74
Hölderin, Friedrich, 59
Holidays, secular, 57
Holy Roman Empire, 23–24, 24–27, 28, 79

I

Immigrants, 53, 88
Imports, 49

INDEX

Income, 83–84
Industry, 46
Infant mortality rate, 9
Information technology, 45
Infrastructure, 46, 50, 86
Institutions, cultural, 86–87
International
    Car of the Year, 45
    Modern style, 60
Iron Chancellor. *See* Bismarck, Otto von
Islam, 9, 53
Islands, 11
Italy, 26, 49, 53
    alliance with, 34

J
Japan
    agreement with, 34
    Pearl Harbor attack, 35
Jews, murder of, 34
Judaism, 34, 53

K
Kaffe und kuchen, 56
Kaiser, 30
Kaub, 17
Kollwitz, Käthe, 62, 63

L
Lake Constance, 14, 16, 78, 80
Lakes, 16
Länder, 36
Landscape, 11–12, 14
Language, 9
Lietzenburg, 32
Lignite, 47
Lindau, 78, 80, 81
Literacy rate, 9
Literature, 59
Lowlands, 11
Lucas Cranach the Elder, 27
Lufthansa, 45, 48
Luther, Martin, 27, 59
Lutheranism, 27–28
Luxembourg, 7, 11, 26, 35, 40

M
Maastricht Treaty, 40
Magdeburger Reiter, 25
Main river, 16, 82
Mangturm Tower, 81
Mann, Thomas, 59
Manufacturing, 45
Map, 6
Marcks, Gerhard, 77
Marienplatz, 71
Martin Luther (Lucas Cranach the Elder), 27
Mendelssohn, Felix, 59
Mercedes, 55
Merger Treaty, 40
Merkel, Angela, 36, 88
Migration rate, 9
Military, rebuilding, 34
Mittagessen, 56
Moscow, 35
Mountains, 11
Munich, 44, 57, 67, 70–73
    Oktoberfest, 70
Münstertal, 10
Museum
    Island, 66, 67
    Ostwall, 86
Museums, 43, 66, 67, 73, 76, 79, 86, 87
Music, 59

N
Napoleon Bonaparte (David), 28
Nationalism, 28
National Socialist German Workers Party. *See* Nazi Party
Nazi Party, 34
    growth of, 34
Nazis, 30, 34–37
Neckar river, 14, 16
Netherlands, 7, 11, 16, 26, 40, 49
Neue Nationalgalerie, 87
Neuendorf bei Wilster, 7
Neuschwanstein Castle, 22

Nobel Prize for Literature, 59
North
    German Plain, 11–12
    Rhine-Westphalia, 67, 84
    Sea, 7, 8, 11, 13
Norway, 35
Nymphenburg, 72

O
Oder river, 16
Oktoberfest, 44, 57, 70
Olympics, 73
Olympic Village, 73
Otto 1, 24, 25, 26

P
Palatinate, 42
Paris, 30
Parliament, 30, 36
Partition, 36
Peace of Westphalia, 28
Pearl Harbor, 35
Peasants, 27–28
Peasants' War, 27–28
Pharmaceutical industry, 46
Pied Piper of Hamlin, 59
"Pivot of Europe," 11
Planck, Max, 54
Poland, 7, 11, 27, 35, 49
    and World War II, 35
Population, 9, 53
    age, 9
    growth rate, 9
Pork hock with sauerkraut, 56
Porsche, 43, 46
    911, 45
    Museum, 43
Praying Woman (Kollwitz), 62
Princip, Gavrilo, 30
Protestantism, 9, 27–28, 53
Prussia, 28, 31, 32

R
Realschule, 54
Recipes, 57
Reformation, 27–28

INDEX

Reichstag, 30
   building, 38
   Hitler address to, 35
Religion, 9, 53
   freedom of, 53
Reparation, 30
Revolt, 27–28
Rhine
   river, 14, 15, 16
   Valley, 17
Rhineland-Palatinate, 15
Rhine-Ruhr area, 74–75
Rivers, 14–16
Rococo, 32
Rohe, Ludwig Mies van der, 61
Roma (Gypsies), 53
Roman
   Catholicism, 9, 26, 27–28, 53
   Empire. See Holy Roman Empire
Romanesque Revival style, 22
Romans, 23
Rosberg, Nico, 55
Ruhr, 51
Russia, 30

S
Sauerkraut, 56
Sausage, 56
Saxons, 24
Schering, 46
Schiller, Friedrich, 59
Schinkel, Karl Friedrich, 32
Schleswig-Holstein Wadden Sea National Park, 13
Schlüter, Andreas, 32
Schoenburg, Arnold, 59
Schubert, Franz, 59
Schultüte, 57
Schumann, Robert, 59
Schwanzer, 73
Service sector, 45, 50
Sheep, 12
Siemens, 46
Sisters of St. Joseph of St.

Trudpert, 10
Slovenia, 26
Soccer, 54
Sophie Charlotte, 32
Sorbs/Wends, 53
South German Hills, 12
Soviet Union, 36
   invasion of, 35
   pact, 35
Spandau Forest, 32
Speicherstadt, 68
Sports, 54–55
   snow, 14
Spree River, 64
Springerle, 57
St.
   John's Church (Johanneskirche), 53
   Martin's Church, 76
   Trudpert's Abbey, 10
   Viktor's Cathedral, 78
Standard of living, 83–84
Stars and Stripes, 35
States (Länder), 65
Strauss, Richard, 59
Strikes, 36
Stuttgart, 53
Superiority, 34
Switzerland, 7, 11, 14, 26, 49, 78

T
Taxes, 84
Third Reich, 34
Thirty Years' War, 27
Throne of Charlemagne, 26
Thuringian Forest, 12
Tiergarten park, 67
Tourism, 45
Town Musicians of Bremen (Marcks), 77
Transportation, 48
Treaties of Rome, 40
Treaty of Paris, 40
Turkey, 53
TV Tower, 65

U
Unemployment, 49, 50, 84
UNESCO World Heritage Site, 68
Unification, 28, 37, 38, 49
United
   Kingdom, 49
   Nations, 23
   States, 36, 49
Uplands, 11
Urban society, 65
U-Tower, 86

V
Vineyards, 17
Volkswagen, 46
   Beetle, 45

W
Wagner, Richard, 59
War of Liberation, 28
Watteau, 32
Wealth, distribution of, 83
Weill, Kurt, 59
Weimar Republic, 30
Welfare bill, 49
Weser river, 16, 76
Westerheversand Lighthouse, 13
West Germany, 8, 36, 37, 40, 49
Wilhelm
   I, 28, 31, 32
   II, 67
Wine, 42, 56
Woodlands, 19
World Cup, 54
World War
   I, 30
   II, 30, 34–37, 40, 43–44
Wurst, 56

X
Xanten, 78
   Archaeological Park & Roman Museum, 79

Picture Credits

All images in this book are in the public domain or have been supplied under license by © Shutterstock.com. The publisher credits the following images as follows:

Page 16: FooTToo, page 8: Roman Babakin, page 17: Igor Plotnikov, page 26: John Kehly, page 30-31: Karnizz, page 37: Josef Hanus, page 40: Roman Yanushevsky, page 43: Markus Mainka, page 44: Talashi Images, page 48: Vytautas, page 54: rki foto, page 55: Mr Segui, page 58: Mirenska, page 67, 84: Tupungato, page 73 Meaniera, page 75 Shchipkova Elena, page 78: Axel Fischer, page 80: Trabantos, 86: VanReel, page 87 Claudion Divizia Page 88: 360b.

To the best knowledge of the publisher, all images not specifically credited are in the public domain. If any image has been inadvertently uncredited, please notify the publisher, so that credit can be given in future printings.

Video Credits

Page 12 Geography Now!: http://x-qr.net/1Dos
page 24 EmperorTigerstar: http://x-qr.net/1CsX
page 45 DW English: http://x-qr.net/1Fgf
page 55 Studio G: http://x-qr.net/1EB6
page 66 Vidtur: http://x-qr.net/1DYt

Author

Dominic J. Ainsley is a freelance writer on history, geography, and the arts and the author of many books on travel. His passion for traveling dates from when he visited Europe at the age of ten with his parents. Today, Dominic travels the world for work and pleasure, documenting his experiences and encounters as he goes. He lives in the south of England in the United Kingdom with his wife and two children.